SUPER SHEROES OF HISTORY

Ancient Civilizations

Women Who Made a Difference

LORI MCMANUS

Children's Press®
An imprint of Scholastic Inc.

Thank you to Brittany Schulman for her insights into Indigenous Peoples' history and culture.

Picture credits:

Photos ©: cover top: Lebrecht Music & Arts/Alamy Images; cover center bottom: Imaginechina Limited/Alamy Images; cover bottom: Painters/Alamy Images; 5 left: Lebrecht Music & Arts/Alamy Images; 5 center right: Imaginechina Limited/Alamy Images; 5 right: Science History Images/Alamy Images; 6 top: Imaginechina Limited/Alamy Images; 7 top: Chen Xiaobo/TAO Images Limited/Alamy Images; 8 bottom: British Library Board. All Rights Reserved/Bridgeman Images; 9 top: Fandom; 9 bottom: Xinhua/Alamy Images; 10 center: The Granger Collection; 10 bottom: Christie's Images/Bridgeman Images; 11 top: Liu Xiaoyang/China Images/Alamy Images; 11 center: Artokoloro Quint Lox Limited/age fotostock; 12 top: Pictures From History/AGB Photo Library/age fotostock; 16 top: Look and Learn/Bridgeman Images; 17 top: PHAS/Universal Images Group/Getty Images; 18 bottom: incamerastock/Alamy Images; 19 top: James Nesterwitz/Alamy Images; 21 top right: Floriano Rescigno/Alamy Images; 21 bottom right: Peter Horree/Alamy Images; 22 left: Lebrecht Music & Arts/Alamy Images; 24 bottom: 2HPictorial Press Ltd/Alamy Images; 25 top: Museum of London/Heritage Image Partnership Ltd/Alamy Images; 25 center: Lebrecht Authors/Bridgeman Images; 26 top: Ivy Close Images/Alamy Images; 27 top: Historia/Shutterstock; 29 top: ODI/Alamy Images; 30 left: Science History Images/Alamy Images; 31 top: The Holbarn Archive/Bridgeman Images; 31 bottom: Nastasic/Getty Images; 32 top: incamerastock/Alamy Images; 33 top: Look and Learn/Bridgeman Images; 34 top: Sheila Terry/Science Source; 35 top: Bridgeman Images; 35 bottom left: Adolf Gnauth/Wikimedia; 36 top: Historia/Shutterstock; 38 top: Painters/Alamy Images; 38 bottom: Veneranda Biblioteca Ambrosiana/Mondadori Portfolio/Bridgeman Images; 39 all: AGB Photo Library/Pictures From History/age fotostock; 40 top: Wikimedia; 40 bottom: Art Collection 2/Alamy Images; 41 top: Prisma Archivo/Alamy Images; 41 bottom: HeritagePics/Alamy Images; 42 top center: Zev Radovan/BibleLandPictures/Alamy Images; 42 top right: The Art Archive/Shutterstock; 42 bottom left: incamerastock/Alamy Images; 42 bottom center: AYK9FChronicle/Alamy Images; 42 bottom right: Artokoloro/Alamy Images; 43 bottom left: ART Collection/Alamy Images; 43 bottom center: Rudy Canales/Wikimedia; 43 bottom right: Lebrecht Music & Arts/Alamy Images; 44-45: pop_jop/Getty Images.

All other photos © Shutterstock.

Library of Congress Cataloging-in-Publication Data Available

ISBN 978-1-338-84059-9 (library binding) | ISBN 978-1-338-84060-5 (paperback)

10 9 8 7 6 5 4 3 2 1   23 24 25 26 27

Printed in China   62
First edition, 2023

Series produced for Scholastic by Parcel Yard Press

Contents

Who Are the Super SHEroes of History?

Throughout history, women have ruled countries, led soldiers into battle, changed laws, come up with new ways of thinking, and worked to improve life for everyone. Women's actions and ideas have changed the course of history for whole societies, whole countries, and even the whole world. Women have made a difference. Often, however, their achievements have gone unrecognized.

This book celebrates the life and accomplishments of twelve of these women, twelve Super SHEroes of History! They all lived in ancient civilizations in places such as Greece, Rome, Egypt, and China.

Ancient civilizations were well-organized and developed societies from long ago that were the forerunners of later states, nations, and empires.

Boudicca Cleopatra Fu Hao Hypatia

The Super SHEroes in this book wrote influential scientific and poetic works, led military resistance to invaders, and ruled great empires. Some of them were born to positions of privilege while others gained their reputation through courage, intelligence, or by accident. Most of them had to overcome many obstacles in order to make their names, but they were still able to achieve things that made a difference to the times in which they lived.

This book brings the stories of these Super SHEroes to you! And while you read them, remember:

Your story can make a difference, too. You can become a Super SHEro of History!

Fu Hao

Fu Hao's tomb was discovered in China in 1976. The **artifacts** inside revealed that Fu Hao was a military general and priestess who changed the course of history.

Fu Hao lived during the Shang Dynasty in China around 3,000 years ago. She married King Wu Ding as an agreement of loyalty between her tribe and the king. Fu Hao was one of sixty-four royal wives. She was determined to stand out from the crowd.

This is an old partial map of an ancient Chinese empire. Fu Hao had a good knowledge of China's geography.

datafile

Born: c. 1273 BCE

Died: c. 1240 BCE

Place of birth: China

Role: General and priestess

Super SHEro for: Commanding an army and being an important religious leader

A chariot design used in China during the Shang Dynasty

The king took Fu Hao with him on a three-year tour of his kingdom. Fu Hao learned the geography of China. She also sharpened her military skills. Soon, a tribe called the Tu invaded Shang territory from the north. Fu Hao volunteered to lead the battle against them. She fought hard, inspired her troops, and won.

Fu Hao also defeated the Qiang in the northwest and the Yi in the south. Next she fought the Ba tribe from the southwest alongside her husband. Fu Hao tricked the Ba by sending soldiers to attack the Ba's neighbors. When the Ba army left its homeland to help, it was trapped and destroyed by Fu Hao's waiting forces.

Fu Hao was also a priestess. Only the most powerful rulers in China held this job. During the Shang Dynasty, people believed in a main god called Di, and in many nature gods. People also thought they needed help from their dead ancestors to communicate with the gods. Fu Hao led religious ceremonies to ask the spirits of the ancestors for guidance.

Fu Hao wrote questions for the gods on tortoise shells or ox bones. She baked the hard shells or bones until they cracked. Then Fu Hao studied the cracks carefully. The patterns were supposed to contain **oracles** from the gods about the future. Fu Hao figured out the messages and announced them.

An oracle bone with Chinese writing from the time of the Shang Dynasty

8

People asked the gods and ancestors about personal problems, such as how to get rid of a toothache. Others requested oracles for issues important to the whole nation. The royal family looked for guidance about winning wars, preventing natural disasters, and growing large amounts of food.

Sometimes Fu Hao made **sacrifices** to the gods. This was common during the Shang Dynasty. The priestess hoped the sacrifices would please the gods and convince them to bless the people with happiness and protection.

In the mid-1200s BCE, Fu Hao was the most powerful woman in China.

Did You Know?

Fu Hao carried a large, decorated bronze axe into battle. It weighed around 20 pounds (9 kg). Fu Hao probably would not have been able to fight with such a heavy weapon. Instead, she carried it as a sign that she was the person in charge.

Fu Hao's tomb is near the modern city of Anyang in Henan, China.

Not long after Fu Hao's victory over the Ba tribe, she became sick and died at the young age of thirty-three. Wu Ding honored Fu Hao by burying her in a tomb built only for her. Many Chinese royal tombs were robbed over the centuries. However, Fu Hao's tomb was forgotten. It remained untouched until **archaeologists** found it in 1976. They were amazed at what they saw inside.

A Shang axe head with a face pattern

Shang Dynasty jugs often had the shape of animals.

Fu Hao was buried with many treasures. There were 700 items of **jade**, mostly carved into animal shapes like birds, dragons, tigers, and owls. The tomb contained 560 bone hairpins and arrowheads. There were even 6,000 seashells. The largest items were cast from bronze.

The 4,000 bronze objects included, bells, mirrors, and weapons. Large bronze axes showed Fu Hao's name and rank. Sixteen servants were also buried in the tomb with Fu Hao!

This tomb was very unusual for a woman in ancient China, even the wife of a king. Most female members of the royal family were buried with their husbands or ancestors. **Fu Hao earned special treatment because she was such a smart and strong military general and a powerful priestess.**

Fu Hao's tomb contained the bones of servants who would look after her after death.

A bowl used in Shang religious rituals

What Would You Do?

Fu Hao performed religious ceremonies to ask the gods and ancestors for guidance about military battles.

How would you have gained guidance for the nation?

Who or what would you rely on for advice and help?

Life in the Times of Fu Hao
CHINA: 1200s BCE

During the Shang Dynasty, women were not usually the leaders giving orders to men. They were supposed to obey their husbands and be calm, gentle, and respectful. A woman's most important role was taking care of her children and home.

King Cheng Tang started the Shang Dynasty around 1600 BCE.

Women didn't choose their husbands in those days. Parents arranged a marriage for a daughter when she was around fourteen or fifteen years old. Sometimes poor parents sold a daughter as a servant to a rich family instead. The girl had no say in the matter!

Girls learned how to prepare food, look after children, and clean a home.

Spinning

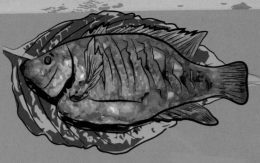

Simple meals

They might also learn how to spin yarns, weave cloth, and sew. Only the sons of rich parents went to school. Wealthy girls sometimes learned to read and write at home.

As a wealthy woman, Fu Hao likely lived in a large wooden house. But most families lived in one- or two-room huts with mud walls, straw roofs, dirt floors, and very little furniture. They ate simple food such as wheat pancakes or rice and fish if they lived near a river.

Bronze was the main metal in Fu Hao's time.

Two statuettes from the Shang Dynasty

Cleopatra

Cleopatra ruled Egypt, one of the oldest and most wealthy civilizations in the ancient world. However, she lived in a dangerous time and used clever thinking to stay in power.

SUPER SHEROES OF HISTORY

Cleopatra came from a long line of kings and queens who had ruled Egypt for more than 200 years. Egypt was powerful, but the Romans across the sea in Italy were getting stronger and threatened Egypt. Cleopatra's father was the king. Growing up, she knew she would be the leader one day.

The pyramids of Giza were already thousands of years old when Cleopatra ruled Egypt.

datafile

Born: c. 69 BCE

Died: 30 BCE

Place of birth: Egypt

Role: Queen

Super SHEro for: Ruling her kingdom with intelligence and skill

Cleopatra ruled from the city of Alexandria, which had a huge lighthouse at the mouth of the Nile River.

That day came when Cleopatra's father died in 51 BCE. Cleopatra and her younger brother Ptolemy XIII took over as joint rulers of Egypt. She was eighteen years old, and he was just ten.

The sister and brother were supposed to govern together. Instead, they fought each other for control. Cleopatra made important decisions, but her brother and his advisers disagreed with her. They drove her out of the country. Cleopatra formed an army and returned to fight against her brother's troops.

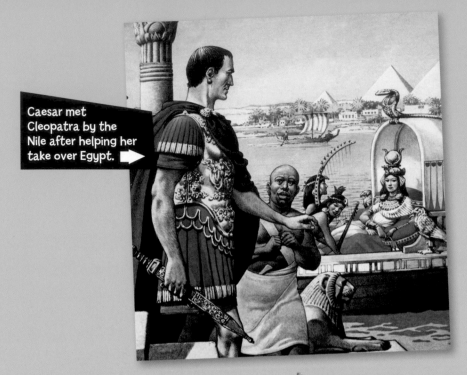

Caesar met Cleopatra by the Nile after helping her take over Egypt.

Meanwhile, the Roman leader Julius Caesar arrived in Egypt. Cleopatra sneaked into Caesar's quarters to ask him to help her defeat her brother.

Caesar decided to make a deal with Cleopatra. He would help her take over Egypt, and in return Cleopatra would pay for the Roman leader's military conquests. After six months of fighting, the pair drove the army of Ptolemy XIII out of Alexandria, and the young king drowned in the Nile River. Caesar announced that Cleopatra was Egypt's queen.

Julius Caesar ➡

This ancient Egyptian carving shows Caesar (left) and Cleopatra (right), with their son, Caesarion.

Cleopatra and Caesar also began a love affair. Cleopatra gave birth to a son. He was called Caesarion, or "little Caesar." Julius Caesar and Cleopatra moved to Rome. She stayed at Caesar's luxurious home. Caesar had a golden statue of Cleopatra made to show off her beauty and importance.

Some Roman leaders thought Caesar was becoming too powerful. They murdered him in a sudden attack. Cleopatra fled back to Egypt.

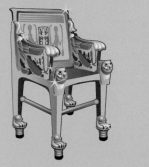

Did You Know?

Cleopatra was extremely smart and capable. She commanded an army and a navy, wrote essays about science and medicine, and spoke at least ten languages. Cleopatra also helped set up a system of coinage in Egypt and strengthened the country's **economy**.

Caesar's allies and enemies went to war for control of Rome. Cleopatra sent troops to help Caesar's allies, who were victorious. Caesar's adopted son, Octavian, and a general named Mark Antony became Rome's new leaders.

Cleopatra was worried that one of them might try to take over Egypt, so she decided to make a pact with Antony. Antony agreed to protect Egypt and allow Cleopatra to continue as queen. Antony and Cleopatra also started a love affair. They had three children together. They planned eventually to have their family rule all of Rome's and Egypt's lands.

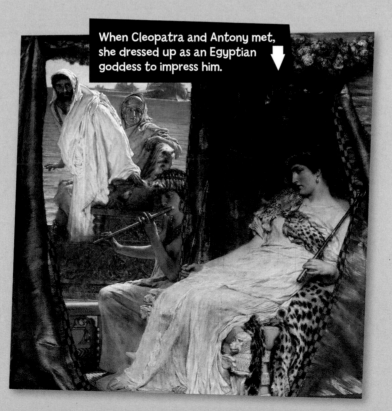

When Cleopatra and Antony met, she dressed up as an Egyptian goddess to impress him.

When Octavian learned of this plan, he declared war on Cleopatra and invaded Egypt. He won a victory at the naval Battle of Actium. Antony killed himself after hearing a rumor that Cleopatra was dead. To avoid capture, Cleopatra killed herself, too. She may have drunk poison. One story says that she held a poisonous snake so it would bite her.

Egypt fell under Roman control. Cleopatra had ruled her kingdom skillfully for two decades. **She was the last ruler of ancient Egypt—and is one of the most famous women in history.**

After his victory at Actium, Octavian became ruler of Rome under the title Emperor Augustus.

What Would You Do?

Cleopatra built alliances with other leaders in order to protect Egypt from invasion.

Do you think working with other countries was a good idea?

Or would you have tried to remain independent?

Life in the Times of Cleopatra
EGYPT: First Century BCE

In the days of Cleopatra, women with time and wealth paid special attention to their appearance. They bathed up to four times a day!

Wigs made of real hair

Women often cut their own hair short to stay cool and clean in the hot climate—and then wore wigs on top. The wigs were made of real hair arranged in braids, strands, and curls.

Women liked to enhance their appearance with makeup. They used black powder eyeliner around their eyes. This made their eyes look bigger. The eyeliner also reduced the glare of the sun and kept insects away. Women painted color on their eyelids, eyebrows, cheeks, and lips, too. They also used strong-smelling perfumes.

Black powder eyeliner

Egyptian women are said to have bathed in donkey milk! The sour liquid was good for their skin.

Wealthy women wore jewelry such as bracelets, rings, earrings, necklaces, and **amulets**. Their jewelry was made from gold, silver, and precious stones. Pearls were the most expensive jewels of all.

As the queen, Cleopatra was far richer than other women in Egypt. She had jewels sewn onto her sandals and clothes. She even decorated her hair with jewels. Cleopatra had earrings made for her from the two largest pearls in the world. She was said to have dropped one of them into a glass of vinegar, watched it dissolve, and then drank it in front of an audience to show off her wealth.

Many Egyptian women wore long, dark wigs.

Gold bracelet with precious stones from ancient Egypt

Perfumes

Boudicca

Boudicca was queen of the Iceni tribe in southeast Britain. In 60 CE, the Romans suddenly took away her people's lands. Boudicca decided to fight back.

SUPER SHEROES OF HISTORY

Little is known about the early life of Queen Boudicca. She married Prasutagus, king of the Iceni tribe, when she was eighteen years old. At that time, the Romans were trying to take control of all the land in Britain. They often used force to make that happen.

datafile

Born: c. 30 CE

Died: c. 61 CE

Place of birth: Britain

Role: Queen and warrior

Super SHEro for: Fighting Roman invaders so her people could stay independent

Boudicca's people lived in simple round huts.

Prasutagus made a deal with the Romans. He suggested that, after his death, the Iceni kingdom would be divided between the Roman emperor and his two daughters. It didn't work out that way.

Instead, the Romans took control of all the king's property and lands when he died. They refused to let the Iceni people rule part of their own territory. Queen Boudicca objected. To punish her, the Romans beat Boudicca with a whip in front of a crowd. They also hurt her daughters.

The Romans controlled ancient Britain using their powerful army.

Like many women in ancient Britain, Boudicca had trained to be a warrior. She knew how to use weapons. She prepared for war against the Romans. Boudicca called together warriors—men and women—from her own people and from other British tribes. They were all tired of being treated unfairly under Roman rule.

Boudicca's army struck when the Roman governor Suetonius was away. Her troops defeated a strong group of Roman soldiers. Then they destroyed Camulodunum (now Colchester), the first capital city of Roman Britain. Next, Boudicca and her troops headed for the Roman cities of Londinium (now London) and Verulamium (now called St. Albans). They burned the cities to the ground.

Boudicca led her army of ancient Britons from a horse-drawn chariot.

Boudicca and her troops were now in control of the main parts of Roman Britain. They smashed up any Roman art and buildings they came across. Boudicca's plan to wipe out the Romans had worked so far.

Meanwhile, Suetonius returned to the southeast of the country when he heard about Boudicca's victories. He didn't have as many troops as Boudicca. So he carefully chose a location for the next battle.

With Londinium left undefended by the Romans, the Britons burned the city to the ground.

Did You Know?

Boudicca stood out from the crowd. She was very tall with long, reddish hair down to her hips. Boudicca also had a loud, harsh voice. One historian described her appearance as "most terrifying"—though he likely had never met her.

Boudicca's two daughters traveled with her in the chariot.

Suetonius placed his troops in a narrow valley near Watling Street, which was the main road running north from Londinium. His army had woods behind it and hills on either side. This meant that if Boudicca's forces wanted to attack, they would have to do it from the front. They would have nowhere to hide.

Boudicca's huge army set up camp along the edge of Watling Street. The warriors even invited their families to watch the fighting. Boudicca drove around in her chariot to urge the warriors to be brave. She cried out, "Win the battle or die! That is what I, a woman, will do."

Watling Street is still there 2,000 years later.

As the Britons charged forward, Suetonius's army began by throwing **javelins** at the warriors. Boudicca had too many fighters gathered in a small space. They made easy targets for the skilled Roman soldiers.

Boudicca's army tried to run away but there was nowhere to go. They were trapped by their own camp. Realizing they had lost, Boudicca and her daughters took poison to kill themselves.

Boudicca lost the Battle of Watling Street that day. **Yet she is known as the warrior queen who fought bravely against the power of Rome.**

Boudicca poisoned herself instead of becoming a prisoner of Rome.

What Would You Do?

The Roman invaders broke their agreement with Boudicca's tribe, so she led them into war.

Would you have worked with the Romans to prevent a war?

Would you step down as a leader if it meant saving lives?

Life in the Times of Boudicca

BRITAIN: First Century CE

The Iceni tribe lived in what is today the East Anglia region of southern England. Before the Romans arrived in Britain, the Iceni were a rich and powerful people. Boudicca was a member of the Iceni royal family.

An Iceni home, inside and out

The Iceni lived as farmers, growing wheat and barley and raising sheep. They lived in round houses built for the rainy weather. The houses had high thatched roofs with holes for letting out the smoke from indoor fire pits. The walls were coated in dried mud and the dung of sheep and horses. The door faced the southeast, toward the rising sun.

Sheep

It is likely that Boudicca and her family lived in a square or rectangular home much larger than most people's, with several rooms. They may also have lived in a walled-off part of the village containing several royal buildings.

The Iceni were skilled metalworkers. Unlike other ancient British tribes, the Iceni used coins as money. Wealthy Iceni people decorated their horses and chariots with elaborate metal harnesses to show how rich they were. Ancient Britons often wore torcs, heavy rings of gold or silver looped around the neck. Perhaps Boudicca wore a magnificent torc when riding her chariot!

Coins

Wheat

29

Hypatia

Hypatia studied and taught mathematics and science at an important college. She earned respect as a scholar and **philosopher**. Her scientific ideas and teaching angered some religious leaders.

Hypatia lived in the city of Alexandria in Egypt. After the death of Cleopatra, Alexandria had become an important city in the Roman Empire. For centuries, Alexandria was the world center for learning. However, that time was coming to an end.

datafile

Born: c. 355 CE

Died: 415 CE

Place of birth: Egypt

Role: Teacher, mathematician, and philosopher

Super SHEro for: Being an expert in mathematics and philosophy and an important teacher

Hypatia believed the sun and the planets went around Earth. So did everyone else back then!

Alexandria had the largest library in the ancient world. Most of the writing was on scrolls.

Hypatia's father, Theon, taught at the college in Alexandria. He studied math and astronomy. Theon educated Hypatia in these subjects. He prepared her to follow in his footsteps at the school. Usually, this would be a role for a scholar's son. But Theon knew Hypatia could do the job just as well.

Hypatia had a brilliant mind. She helped her father write complex explanations about geometry, algebra, and the way the planets moved. Hypatia also wrote her own scientific papers. She became an expert at designing **astrolabes**.

An astrolabe measures the positions of stars.

31

Hypatia became a famous teacher in Alexandria.

Hypatia was a very good philosophy teacher. She blended together the ideas of several ancient Greek philosophers, such as Plato and Aristotle.

Hypatia also gave many public lectures. On these occasions, she wore the special robes usually worn only by male scholars. She made difficult ideas easy to understand. People crowded in to hear her, and many scholars were eager to learn from her. Some traveled great distances to hear Hypatia talk about philosophy and math. But not everyone liked Hypatia's teachings.

When speaking in public, Hypatia wore the same clothes as the male teachers.

At that time, the Christian religion was becoming more popular. Hypatia was not a Christian. Her belief system was based on ideas from before the time of Jesus. Some church leaders thought Hypatia's teachings would stop people from accepting the Christian faith.

Alexandria's bishop, Cyril, was not happy with Hypatia's popularity. Besides that, Hypatia was a close friend of Orestes, the Roman governor of Egypt. The bishop and the governor were rivals. They both wanted to control Alexandria. Hypatia suffered because of this conflict.

Did You Know?

Hypatia chose not to get married so she could devote herself to learning and teaching. Hypatia gained respect for her knowledge, good judgment, and dedication. She influenced the people and belief systems in Alexandria.

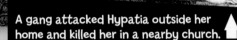

A gang attacked Hypatia outside her home and killed her in a nearby church. ⬆

A rumor spread that Hypatia tried to stop Orestes and Cyril from settling their disagreements. An angry **mob** of Christians dragged Hypatia from her chariot, killed her, and burned her body. **After her tragic death, Hypatia was recognized around the world as an important philosopher and brilliant teacher. Her ideas have been discussed and studied ever since.**

What Would You Do ?

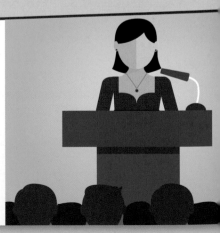

Hypatia kept teaching publicly even when powerful people disagreed with her.

What would you do if you felt pressured to stop or change your favorite activity?

Would you give in because others disagreed with you?

Life in the Times of Hypatia

EGYPT: 4th Century

Many books were lost forever when Alexandria's library was set alight.

Alexandria experienced a devastating **tsunami** around the time of Hypatia's birth. The powerful wave destroyed about 50,000 homes. It hurt businesses and killed thousands of people. The shoreline changed, and seawater swamped some of the royal buildings. At the same time, disagreement between religious groups and the Roman government was increasing.

Public violence became more common. Christian fighters destroyed Alexandria's library and many large temples. The city's college was eventually shut down. Hypatia's father, Theon, was one of its last leaders. Alexandria lost its position as a great center of learning.

Tsunami

SUPER SHEROES OF HISTORY

Hatshepsut

Very few women rose to become **pharaohs** in ancient Egypt. Hatshepsut accomplished this and added a unique twist. She ruled as a king! Statues sometimes show her in the clothing and false beard of a male pharaoh.

To begin with, Hatshepsut ruled alongside her half-brother Thutmose II. When Thutmose died, Hatshepsut had herself crowned with the full powers of a pharaoh. Her greatest achievement was building a vast temple at Deir el-Bahri near her capital city, Thebes. Hatshepsut also traded with other countries and made Egypt very rich.

Hatshepsut
(Egypt, c. 1507-1458 BCE)

Sappho

Sappho was a famous poet in ancient Greece. She lived on the island of Lesbos and ran a school for girls. She taught writing, singing, and poetry performance. In Sappho's day, people often sang poems a little like songs.

Sappho developed new, influential ways of writing **lyric** poetry. Sappho wrote honestly about love, jealousy, and hatred. Her words and phrases were direct and beautiful. She even invented a new rhythmic pattern known today as the Sapphic meter. Sadly, most of Sappho's poems have been lost over time.

Sappho
(Greece, c. 610–570 BCE)

SUPER SHEROES OF HISTORY

Zenobia

Zenobia began her reign as queen of Palmyra in what is now Syria in about 268 CE. The queen and her troops invaded most of the eastern half of the Roman Empire. Then Zenobia declared herself as an **empress** independent of Rome. However, the Roman emperor quickly defeated Zenobia's army and took her as a prisoner.

Zenobia
(Palmyra, c. 240-274 CE)

Helena

Helena
(Greece, c. 248-328 CE)

Around 272 CE, Greek-born Helena gave birth to the future Roman emperor Constantine I. Both Constantine and Helena became Christians and helped spread the faith. In her seventies, Helena traveled to the **Holy Land**, gathering Christian **relics**. Today, the Orthodox and Roman Catholic churches consider Helena a saint.

Wu Zetian

Wu Zetian was born in 624 to a wealthy family during the Tang Dynasty in China. During this part of ancient Chinese history, women had more freedom than before. They could play sports and wear male clothing.

The emperor of China married Wu, who acted like a gentle, respectful wife in public. Behind the scenes, Wu Zetian was the real ruler of China. During her reign as empress, Wu Zetian took decisive action. She organized a secret police force and a system of spies to take care of plots against the empire. She got rid of government employees who were not doing their jobs well. Wu's troops also conquered new lands for China.

Wu Zetian
(China, 624-705 CE)

Polo, a ball game played on horseback, was popular among wealthy Tang women. ➡️

39

Ancient Civilizations MAYA

Wak Chanil Ajaw

Wak Chanil Ajaw was one of the few women to become a Mayan leader. She is also known as Lady Six Sky. She became queen of the Mayan kingdom of Naranjo in what is now Guatemala in 682 CE. Later on, Wak Chanil Ajaw reigned with her son. They put up many carved monuments called stelas to record their important actions and ancestry.

A stela of Wak Chanil Ajaw (Guatemala, died 741 CE)

Mama Ocllo Coya (Peru, 1400s CE)

Mama Ocllo Coya

Ancient Civilizations INCA

Mama Ocllo Coya grew up as a princess in the Inca Empire in what is now Peru. She married her brother Topa Inca Yupanqui, who became emperor in 1471. As empress, Mama Ocllo gave him wise advice and helped him advance the Inca Empire. She was a brilliant strategist who was known for her good judgment.

Malintzin

Malintzin
(Mexico, c. 1500–1529 CE)

Malintzin was born in what is now Mexico to a chief of the Nahua people. However, when Malintzin was about ten, her father died, and she was sold into slavery. She had many different owners and learned Yucatec and Nahuatl, the languages of the Mayan and Aztec people.

In 1519 the Spanish invader Hernán Cortés found out about Malintzin's language skills. Still enslaved, she became his personal translator and some of the letters he received were directly addressed to her. Malintzin helped Cortés defeat the Aztecs, which allowed Spain to take over Mexico. Malintzin became free when she married a Spanish nobleman. She had two children who were among the first **mestizos**.

Malintzin met Cortés as he led a war against the Aztecs.

41

Super SHEroes of History

Timeline
Here are some highlights in the lives of Super SHEroes of ancient civilizations.

Fu Hao uses smart military strategy to defeat the Ba tribe.

The pyramids of Giza were being built in Egypt.

Sappho has written nine books of poetry by the time she dies in this year.

Warrior queen Boudicca leads an uprising against the Romans

| c. 2325 BCE | c. 1473 BCE | 1240s BCE | 776 BCE | c. 570 BCE | 41 BCE | 60 CE | 270 CE |

Hatshepsut becomes the first female Egyptian pharaoh.

First recorded Olympic Games take place in ancient Greece.

Cleopatra forms an alliance with the Roman general Mark Antony.

Zenobia seizes control of much of the eastern Roman Empire.

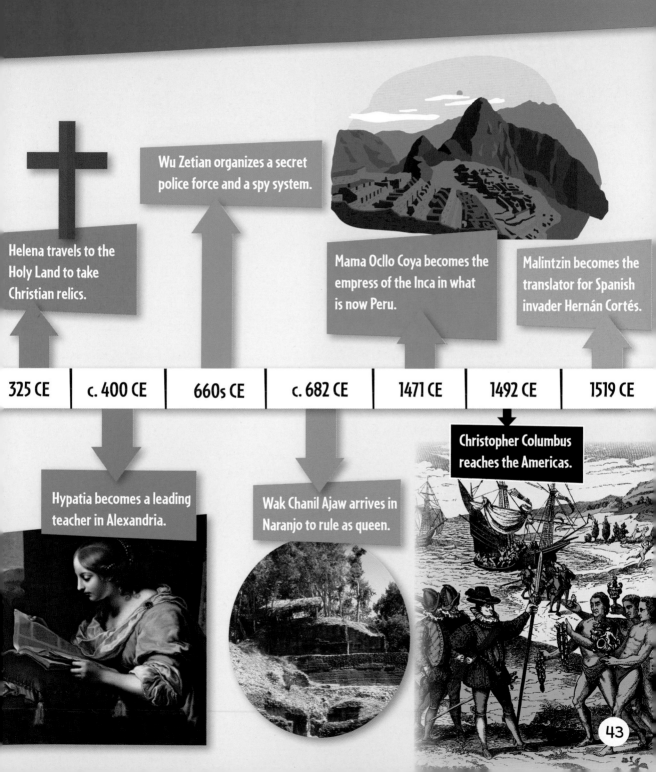

Wu Zetian organizes a secret police force and a spy system.

Helena travels to the Holy Land to take Christian relics.

Mama Ocllo Coya becomes the empress of the Inca in what is now Peru.

Malintzin becomes the translator for Spanish invader Hernán Cortés.

| 325 CE | c. 400 CE | 660s CE | c. 682 CE | 1471 CE | 1492 CE | 1519 CE |

Christopher Columbus reaches the Americas.

Hypatia becomes a leading teacher in Alexandria.

Wak Chanil Ajaw arrives in Naranjo to rule as queen.

1. Boudicca
East Anglia, England
In southeast England, the warrior queen Boudicca and her troops fought fiercely against the Romans.

2. Cleopatra
Rome, Italy
After she had taken control of Egypt, Cleopatra moved to Rome to live with the Roman ruler Julius Caesar.

3. Fu Hao
Yinxu, China
Fu Hao used her knowledge of Chinese geography to win battles. She lived in a capital near the current-day city of Anyang.

4. Hatshepsut
Deir el-Bahri, Egypt
As pharaoh, Hatshepsut oversaw the building of a magnificent temple near the Nile River.

5. Helena
Constantinople
Based in Constantinople (now the city of Istanbul, Turkey), Helena built churches and promoted Christianity.

6. Hypatia
Alexandria, Egypt
Hypatia devoted herself to studying, writing, and teaching in the great city of Alexandria.

North America

Atlantic Ocean

Pacific Ocean

7. 10.

8.

South America

N

7. Malintzin
Tenochtitlan
Malintzin worked for the Spanish invaders who conquered the Aztec capital city (now Mexico City).

8. Mama Ocllo Coya
Cusco, Peru
Mama Ocllo Coya gave wise advice and helped her husband govern the Inca Empire in Peru. The empire's capital was the mountain city of Cusco.

10. Wak Chanil Ajaw
Naranjo, Guatemala
As a Mayan queen, Wak Chanil Ajaw erected several stelas in her kingdom in what is now northern Guatemala.

11. Wu Zetian
Shendu, China
Based in this ancient capital near the modern city of Luoyang, Wu Zetian expanded the Chinese Empire into Central Asia and Korea.

9. Sappho
Lesbos, Greece
Sappho wrote beautiful lyric poetry while teaching at a school on the island of Lesbos in the Aegean Sea.

12. Zenobia
Palmyra, Syria
Zenobia ruled as queen of Palmyra, a kingdom in what is now part of Syria. She then took over the eastern part of the Roman Empire.

Glossary

alliance (uh-**lye**-uhns) a formal agreement between two or more nations

amulet (**am**-yuh-lit) a small object worn for protection from evil

archaeologist (ahr-kee-**ah**-luh-jist) an expert who studies how people lived in ancient times

artifact (**ahr**-tuh-fakt) an object made by humans, like tools or jewelry

astrolabe (**as**-troh-layb) an ancient handheld instrument used for measuring the position of stars and planets in the sky

chariot (**char**-ee-uht) a two-wheeled battle vehicle pulled by horses

dynasty (**dye**-nuh-stee) a long sequence of rulers from the same family

economy (i-**kah**-nuh-mee) the system for making, selling, and buying goods and services

empress (**em**-pris) a female ruler of an empire

geography (jee-**ah**-gruh-fee) the natural features of a place, like rivers and mountains

Holy Land (**hoh**-lee land) lands of ancient Palestine that include Jewish, Christian, and Islamic religious sites

jade (jayd) a hard, blue-green stone that can be carved and polished to make ornaments and jewelry

javelin (**jav**-uh-lin) a light, long spear used for war or in hunting

lyric (**lir**-ik) words that are good for being set to music and sung

mestizo (meh-**stee**-zoh) a person of mixed race, especially one having European and Native American ancestry

mob (mahb) a crowd looking to attack

oracle (**ah**-ruh-kuhl) a message from the gods, usually about the future

pharaoh (**fair**-oh) the highest ruler in ancient Egypt

philosopher (fuh-**lah**-suh-fur) a person who studies ideas about knowledge, truth, and the meaning of life

relic (**rel**-ik) an object from a holy person of the past

sacrifice (**sak**-ruh-*fise*) the act of killing a person or animal in a religious ceremony to please a god

tsunami (tsu-**nah**-mee) a very large sea wave caused by an earthquake or volcano erupting underwater

Index

Further Reading

Alvear Schecter, Vicky. *Cleopatra Rules! The Amazing Life of the Original Teen Queen.* New York: Boyds Mills Press, 2013.

Alvear Schecter, Vicky. *Warrior Queens: True Stories of Six Ancient Rebels Who Slayed History.* New York: Boyds Mills Press, 2019.

Baum, Margaux, and Susanna Thomas. *Hatshepsut* (Leaders of the Ancient World.) New York: Rosen Publishing, 2017.

Holladay Skelley, Billie. *Hypatia: Ancient Alexandria's Female Scholar.* Springfield, Missouri: Paperback Press, 2021.

About the Author

Lori McManus grew up reading about the lives of women around the world. She even put on plays about them! These days, she writes books and helps students, teachers, and schools improve the way they work. She enjoys laughing, learning, and exploring new places.

About the Consultant

Bonnie Morris grew up in California, North Carolina, and Washington, DC. She earned her PhD in women's history and is the author of nineteen books, including *Women's History For Beginners*, *The Feminist Revolution*, and *What's the Score? 25 Years of Teaching Women's Sports History*. She is also a scholarly adviser to the National Women's History Museum and a historical consultant to Disney Animation. In one of her favorite jobs as a professor, she lived on a ship and went around the world (three times!) teaching for Semester at Sea. She has kept a journal since she was twelve and has filled more than 200 notebooks using a fountain pen.